11/03

THE CHANGING FACE OF
BRAZIL

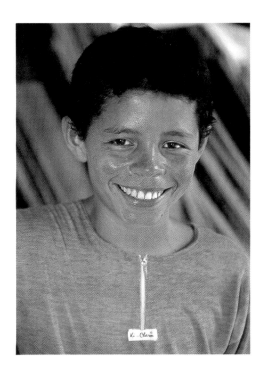

EDWARD PARKER
Author and Photographer

RAINTREE
STECK-VAUGHN
PUBLISHERS

A Harcourt Company

Austin   New York
www.raintreesteckvaughn.com

Published by Raintree Steck-Vaughn Publishers,
an imprint of Steck-Vaughn Company

**Library of Congress Cataloging-in-Publication Data
is available upon request.**

ISBN 0-7398-4965-4

Printed in Italy. Bound in the United States.

1 2 3 4 5 6 7 8 9 0 LB 06 05 04 03 02

Acknowledgments

The publishers would like to thank the following for their
contributions to this book: Nick Hawken – illustrations on
pages 22, 24, 26, 31, 32, 40; Peter Bull – map on page 5. All
photographs are by Edward Parker except: HWPL/Julia
Waterlow 6 (bottom); HWPL/Tony Morrison 35 (middle);
HWPL/Julia Waterlow 38; HWPL/Tony Morrison 39
(bottom); HWPL/Julia Waterlow 41 (top).

Consultant: Gareth Jones, Lecturer in Human Geography at
the London School of Economics and Political Science

Contents

981
PAR
2002

1 "City of Success"

The city of Curitiba began its life in the 17th century as a goldmining town. Standing on a high, flat area of land, it remained a quiet outpost for many years. Cowboys from the southern state of Rio Grande do Sul used to stop and rest there on their way up to São Paulo.

Curitiba's success story began in the late 19th century. Many Europeans emigrated to Curitiba in search of work. They included people from Poland, Germany, Italy, and Russia.

Coffee plantations were set up at the beginning of the 20th century and they provided plenty of work. Gradually the modern city of today began to take shape.

By 1950 farms were also flourishing around Curitiba. Soy and beef are still the city's main produce.

Curitiba is now the capital of the state of Paraná and has a population of over 1.5 million. It is one of Brazil's busiest and fastest-growing cities.

▶ *This map shows the main states, cities, and landscape features of Brazil.*

▲ *Public transportation in Curitiba is cheap and efficient. This means that fewer people drive cars so the city has less pollution and traffic congestion.*

Living standards are high in Curitiba. It is a clean city with good health and education services. There is an efficient public transportation system. The crime rate is low compared to many places in Brazil. The city has plenty of parks, gardens, and pedestrian-only streets. Its historic buildings have been well kept.

These benefits are the result of good planning by local government. Some of the major car manufacturers decided to open factories in Curitiba because the city is so well–managed. They include Volvo, Renault, and Chrysler.

BRAZIL: KEY FACTS

Area: 3,300,232.5 square miles (8,547,403.5 sq km)

Population: 164 million (1999 estimate)

Population density: 49.7 people per square mile (19.18 people per sq km)

Capital: Brasilia (1.9 million)

Other main cities: São Paulo (10 million), Rio de Janeiro (5.6 million), Salvador (2.3 million), Belo Horizonte (2.1 million), Fortaleza (2.1 million), Curitiba (1.6 million)

Highest mountain: Pico da Neblina 9,888 feet (3,014 m)

Longest river: Amazon River 3,899 miles (6,275 km)

Main language: Portuguese

Major religion: Christianity (Catholicism)

Currency: Real

2 Past Times

In the year 1500, a Portuguese sailor named Pedro Alvares set out on a journey to India. He was caught in a storm and his ship was blown off course. He landed on what he thought was an island, and named it Ilha de Vera Cruz. It was, in fact, a vast country that later became known as Brazil.

The Portuguese soon discovered that Brazil was rich in gold. Over the next 100 years they forced many of the native people to work as slaves. More slaves were brought from Africa to work in the gold mines. Europeans rushed to Brazil in the hope of striking it rich. Some succeeded, but many others faced poverty and hardship. In 1822, Brazil gained its independence from Portugal, but the huge gap between rich and poor remained.

Early in the 20th century, there was a growing demand for rubber around the world. Brazil had large supplies of rubber in its Amazon rain forest. Many landowners made vast sums of money from this natural resource, but tens of thousands of

▲ *These schoolgirls are standing below a giant clock in Manaus. It was erected to celebrate the 500 years of history since Brazil was first discovered by Europeans.*

◄ *Ouro Prêto is a mining town in the state of Minas Gerais. Gold was first discovered there in 1698.*

people who came to the rain forest in search of work died from starvation and disease.

Brazil relied heavily upon imported goods until World War II (1939–1945). Supplies from abroad were stopped during the war and new industries had to be developed. Money was put into building new roads and factories. Foreign companies were encouraged to open factories to make cars and other products. The economy began to grow rapidly, but not all Brazilians benefited from the money that was generated by new industries. There is still a huge divide between rich and poor throughout the country.

▼ *The whole city of Brasilia was built in 1950 as part of the plan to develop the economy.*

IN THEIR OWN WORDS

"My name is Sabastiao Teciera Mendes and I am a *seringero* (rubber tapper). I live in the Chico Mendes Extractive Reserve near the small town of Xapuri in the Amazon state of Acre. Here I am collecting rubber latex. My ancestors moved to the Amazon during the rubber boom at the end of the 19th century. They were hoping for a better life, but instead suffered great hardship for nearly one hundred years. The Reserve where I live is named after my cousin, Chico Mendes. He fought for workers' rights, but the lives of seringeros in Acre did not get better until after he died. Once, seringeros were forced to work for no money. Today we have our own cooperative to sell the rubber latex."

3

Landscape and Climate

Brazil is a massive country. Its 3,300,232 square miles (8,547,403 square km) take up almost half of the South American continent. It contains the largest area of tropical rain forest in the world, and has the longest continuous coastline of any country. Brazil is so large that there are still undiscovered mountain ranges and rivers within it.

Brazil is divided into five main regions: the Amazon basin, the River Plate basin, the Guianan Highlands, the Brazil Highlands (also called the Planalto), and the coastal strip.

▼ *The Amazon rain forest covers around 40 percent of Brazil's landscape.*

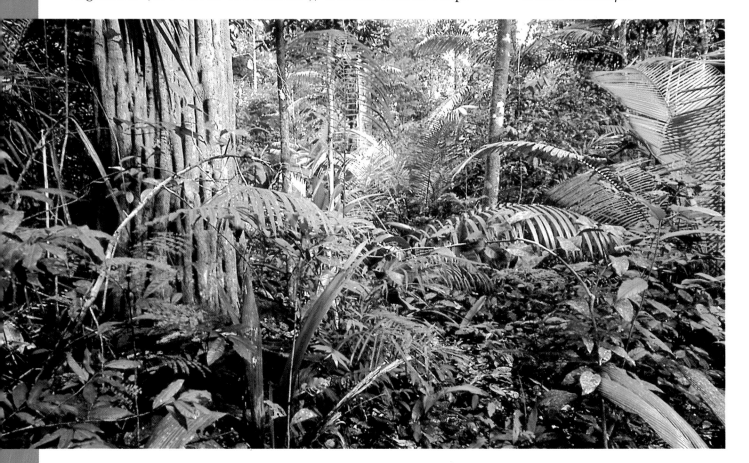

Amazon Basin

The Amazon basin is an enormous valley in northwest Brazil. It was once part of a large inland sea. Most of the region is less than 820 feet (250 m) high and much of it is below sea level. Rain forest covers most of the land, and large areas of it are flooded every year.

The Amazon River runs through this basin. Over 1,100 rivers and streams flow into the Amazon. It carries almost one-fifth of the world's fresh water.

Many people believe the Amazon basin is the hottest part of Brazil, but this is not true. Its climate is constant, with rain every month and an average temperature of 80.6°F (27°C) all year.

Guianan Highlands

The Guianan Highlands run along the northern edge of Brazil. This area is part forest and part arid land. It includes Brazil's tallest mountain, Pico da Neblina with the height of 9,888 feet (3,014 m). This region has distinct wet and dry seasons.

▲ *The water level in the Varzea area of the Flooded Forest rises and falls by 42 feet (13 m) between the wet and dry seasons.*

IN THEIR OWN WORDS

"My name is Neilson Santos da Souza. I live in San Miguel near Sanatrem on the Amazon River. San Miguel is a village that is on Ituqui Island in the Flooded Forest. The water level in the Flooded Forest changes a great deal between the wet and dry seasons each year. The power of the current has a huge effect on the islands. In ten years, the islands that are here now may have disappeared, or changed shape, or moved. Entirely new islands will also have been created.

"When the river is low we can walk between the houses to visit our friends. We also like to go fishing in the lakes. But when the island is flooded, only our houses are above the water and we have to travel everywhere by boat. The flood water brings mud into our gardens, which makes the ground good for growing *manioc* (cassava)."

◀ *The Pantanal is one of the world's largest wetlands. Pantanal is the Portuguese word for swamp.*

▼ *The Great Escarpment meets the coast at Rio de Janeiro. Here, mountains stand right on the edge of the sea.*

River Plate Basin

The River Plate basin is in southern Brazil and extends into Paraguay and Argentina. It includes the Pantanal wetland. This area is less heavily forested than the Amazon basin and has more open grassland. There is a big contrast between the seasons here: winter temperatures fall below 32°F (0°C) and summer temperatures reach 104°F (40°C).

Coastal Strip

The coastal strip runs south for 4,603 miles (7,408 km) from north of the Equator down to the Tropic of Capricorn. It is sandwiched between the Atlantic coast and a mountain range named the Great Escarpment. Mountains stand on the coast from the southern tip of Brazil all the way up to the state of Bahía. Rio de Janeiro's Sugar Loaf Mountain is part of the Great Escarpment.

Brazilian Highlands

The Brazilian Highlands, or Planalto, form an enormous plateau, which has an average height of 1,640 feet (500 m). It reaches into almost every one of Brazil's states and includes several small mountain ranges, the highest of which is near the mining city of Belo Horizonte.

The *cerrado*, which is a lightly-forested savannah, covers most of this region. To the north of the Planalto, towards the Amazon basin, is dense forest. To the south are grassy prairies. An average of 59 inches (1,500 mm) of rain falls here every year.

▶ *An electrical storm heads across the cerrado. This view is from near the city of Cuiabá in Mato Grosso.*

IN THEIR OWN WORDS

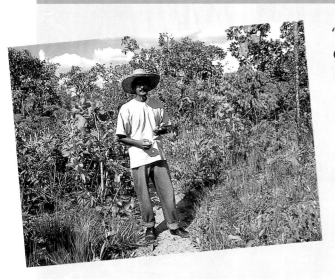

"My name is José Dias de Neto and I live on the Chapado do Guimaraes near the city of Cuiabá in the Center West. I work as a guardian on a cattle ranch in the cerrado. My job is to keep an eye on the cattle. More importantly, I watch out for fires in the dry season. Fires are a natural part of the cerrado but many farmers start them deliberately. They think it improves the grass for the cattle. My boss has a more modern approach. He believes that too much fire is bad for the wild fruit trees and animals, as well as for the soil."

4

Natural Resources

Minerals

Brazil is immensely rich in minerals. There are large supplies of asbestos, bauxite (aluminum ore), copper, chromium, tin, iron, graphite, gold, potassium, and zinc.

Eighteen percent of all the iron ore mined in the world comes from Brazil. The biggest deposits are found in the states of Pará and Minas Gerais. The huge iron ore mine at Grande Carajas in Pará is one of the largest in the world.

Other more rare minerals are also found in Brazil. Ninety percent of the world's supply of niobium comes from Brazil. Niobium is a mineral that is used to make cars. It is mixed with steel and metal alloys to make them lighter and stronger.

▼ *Gold has been mined at Pocone near the city of Cuiabá since the 16th century.*

IN THEIR OWN WORDS

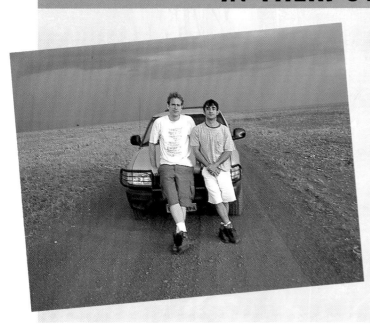

"I am Igor Moustasticoshvily (*left*) pictured here with my personal trainer. I am the general manager of a mineral exploration company, which is based in Cuiabá in the state of Mato Grosso do Norte. Cuiabá was founded when a huge deposit of gold was discovered in a small stream. That spot is now the city center. Gold is still mined at Pocone, only 62 miles (100 km) from Cuiabá. The mining methods used there are outdated. More efficient high-tech methods need to be brought in. Then the mining industry there could have a good future."

Oil

Brazil has major offshore reserves of oil. Its oil fields lie just off the Atlantic coast, near the states of Rio de Janeiro and Espirito Santo in the south-east, and the states of Bahía, Ceará, Rio Grande do Norte, and Sergipe in the northeast. But Brazil managed to produce only 64 percent of the oil it needed in 1998. The rest had to be imported.

A new oil field was discovered off the coast of São Paulo in 1999. It is estimated to contain 600–700 million barrels of oil. Even so, Brazil still has to import oil and natural gas in order to meet its requirements.

▼ *The city of Belém, near the mouth of the Amazon River, has a floating gas station.*

Water

Seventeen percent of all the fresh water on the planet flows through Brazil. This means that there is a huge potential for energy produced from water. Hydroelectric power (HEP) accounted for 43.1 percent of all the energy produced by Brazil in 1998.

The government plans to build more than fifty new HEP plants. The best places for the stations are often thousands of miles away from the cities that need the power. This means that the plans could cause environmental and social problems.

Forests

Brazil's rain forest is the largest in the world. It is valued for more than its wood. Other products include nuts, rubber latex, and palm fruits, from which palm oil is extracted. Tens of thousands of people are employed in harvesting and processing. Rain forest industries generate millions of dollars.

▲ The HEP plant at Itaipu in southern Brazil is the largest in the world. It is downriver from the immensely powerful Iguaçu Falls.

IN THEIR OWN WORDS

"My name is Luis Nelson. I have a farm about 124 miles (200 km) north of Rio de Janeiro. I grow bananas that are dried and sold in Rio. I also have a few hundred cattle. There is a beautiful piece of Atlantic Forest on my land, where there are humming birds, orchids, and other rare species. I made it into a protected reserve, partly because I am very concerned about our water supply.

"The water that flows in the streams and rivers across my land comes from the mountains behind my ranch. Deforestation is causing the area to become drier. The tourist resort of Buzios, which is only 62 miles (100 km) away, completely ran out of water in 1997. The water shortage happened because of deforestation and a change in the local climate."

Southern Brazil has softwood forests and plantation forests containing araucaria pine and eucalyptus trees. Wood from these forests is used in Brazil's massive paper and packaging industries.

Wood has also been used to produce energy. However, this is much less common since 1990, because most of the forests near the cities have already been cut down. Trees were either made into industrial charcoal or chopped into firewood for local people.

Rain forest and plantation wood could be renewable resources if managed well, but logging companies often clear whole areas to make a lot of money quickly. This can destroy these areas of the forest forever.

▼ *This man is working at a sawmill in the state of Bahía. The logs are from a eucalyptus plantation.*

Wildlife

Countless rare plants and animals live in the rain forest. Many of our medicines have come from them. Other forest species probably have undiscovered medicinal uses. There may be vital cures for disease waiting in the rain forest. The government is extremely aware of the potential value of these species. It has banned all research by foreign companies so the profits from any new discoveries are kept within Brazil.

The fish that live in the rivers of the Amazon basin are another valuable resource. Local people catch them to eat. They are also processed for use in a wide range of fish-meat products, including pet food.

Natural Beauty

Brazil's tropical beaches are well-established tourist spots. Ecotourism is also popular. Millions come to the Amazon, and stay in jungle lodges. Others visit the spectacular Iguaçu Falls and the Pantanal, where the wildlife is easier to see than in the Amazon.

▲ *The catch in this boat includes tambaqui and piripitinga, which are popular fish for the local people.*

IN THEIR OWN WORDS

"My name is Rubens Alves. I work as a tourist guide in the Pantanal. Most of the tourists that visit the Pantanal are from the southeast. They like to go fishing and I take them by boat to the best fishing spots.

"I have lived here all my life. In the past I worked as a cowhand on one of the big ranches, but only a few cowhands are needed now."

Most of Brazil's tourists come from other South American countries. Brazil is a favorite with Argentinians, who make up almost half of all tourists. They come because their money is often worth a lot more when it is changed into Brazilian currency. Rates of exchange are very important to Brazil's tourist trade.

Tourism in Brazil has nearly quadrupled from 1.1 million visitors in 1990 to 4 million in 2000. More visitors are beginning to come from Europe, North America, and Asia. Tourism is growing fast and this growth is expected to continue well into the 21st century. Tourism is one of the country's major employers and provided work for 5.8 million people in 1998.

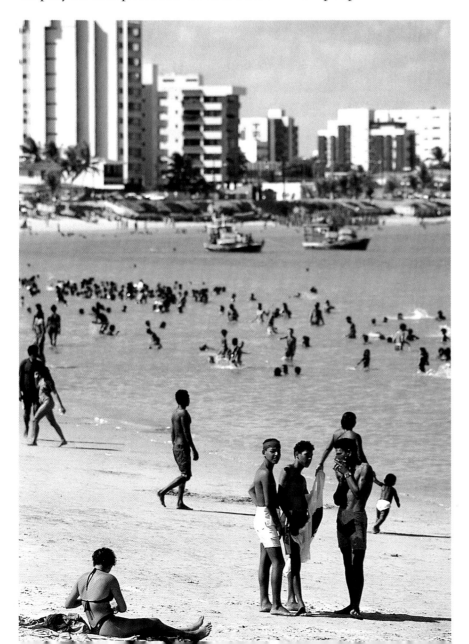

◀ *The resort of Olinda is in the northeast. It is particularly popular with African Brazilians. Brazil's busier beach resorts are suffering from pollution.*

5 The Changing Environment

More than 10 percent of all the world's species live in Brazil. It is home to the jaguar, the giant otter, a quarter of all the world's monkey species, and dozens of types of colorful parrots. There are so many species of plants and insects in Brazil that scientists can only guess at the numbers.

However, all this richness is threatened. The economy and the population of Brazil have grown rapidly since 1970, which has lead to major changes in the environment. Vast areas of the Amazon and other forests have been cut down. Most of the cities now suffer from serious air and water pollution. People are trying to solve the problems in some areas, such as in the city of Curitiba and the Amazonian state of Acre. Imaginative plans are being put into practice to reduce deforestation and urban pollution, but many people in other parts of Brazil are not so forward thinking.

Expansion of Agriculture
The cerrado, in the Brazilian Highlands, is rapidly being converted into farmland. Much of the area is used to produce soy beans, which is an important crop for Brazil.

▼ *This Uakari monkey lives in the Flooded Forest. Its future is threatened because of deforestation in the Amazon.*

Selling soy abroad brings money into Brazil, but this expansion of agriculture is destroying much of the natural landscape. Until recently, the cerrado was not thought to have much environmental value. It is now known to be the home of many rare birds and mammals, such as giant anteaters and maned wolves. Their habitat is severely threatened by agriculture.

The wildlife of the Pantanal is also in danger. Presently, intensive agriculture is not possible because large areas are flooded for half the year. However, it is possible to breed cattle here as they can be moved to higher land during floods. There were three million cattle in the Pantanal in 2000.

▲ *This is the natural cerrado vegetation, near Cuiabá in Mato Grosso do Norte.*

The Hidrovia Plan

A plan to improve farming in the Pantanal was proposed in the 1990s. It has become known as Hidrovia. It suggests that some rivers be straightened and some areas of land drained. This would be good for agriculture, but it would destroy the natural habitat of many species of wildlife. Jaguars live here, as well as over ten million caymans (see photo). The plan is not in motion at the moment because there is no money to pay for it.

Over 270 species of birds exist in the Pantanal. The hyacinth macaw, which is an endangered bird, is found here in greater numbers than anywhere else in the world. The arrival of millions of birds at the start of the wet season is one of the planet's great wildlife spectacles.

▲ *The cayman is a distinct species, related to the alligator. There are many different types of cayman, some of which are threatened with extinction.*

Over Fishing

The Pantanal wetlands provide a habitat for many species of fish. The area is increasingly popular with people who like fishing as a sport. There is growing concern that too many people are coming to fish in the Pantanal and seriously reducing the fish stocks in the area.

IN THEIR OWN WORDS

"My name is Maria Barbosa. Here I am holding a *surubim*, which is a type of catfish found in the Amazon. It may look big, but surubim can grow much larger than this one. I run a hotel in the Pantanal. Most of my customers are fishermen from São Paulo. They come here because the fishing is so good. The number of fishermen that come here has been increasing every year since 1990. I have noticed that the fish they catch are becoming smaller. It also takes them longer to catch a fish than before."

IN THEIR OWN WORDS

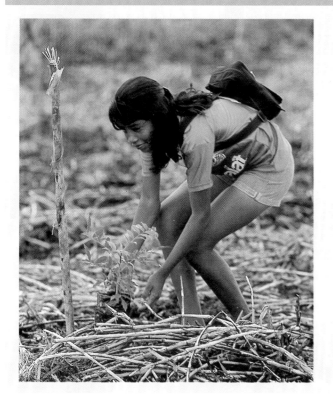

"My name is Isabel Ribeiro Coelho and I am 14 years old. I live in Aracampinas, which is a village near the city of Santarem in the Flooded Forest. Everyone from our village is helping to plant trees today. We are planting these fruit trees on the *restinga* (an area of high ground). In a few years they will produce fruit that fish such as the *tambaqui* and *pirapatinga* like to eat.

"Fishing is very important to our village. We hope that planting these trees will mean that we have more fish in the future. I hope that there will be enough fish for us to continue living here."

Deforestation

Five hundred years ago the Atlantic Forest covered 800,000 square miles (1.3 million square km) of coastal land. Now, less than five percent of this remarkable forest remain. The Amazon rain forest has also been devastated. Sixty percent of the world's rain forests are in Brazil. They cover 2.5 million square miles (4 million square km). The Amazon basin contains the largest remaining rain forest on the planet. Since 1975 the Amazon has experienced massive deforestation. By 1999, forest was being lost at a rate of 10,500 square miles (17,000 square km) each year. This destruction has pushed the Amazon's local people to the edge of extinction. The survival of many species of wildlife is also seriously threatened.

There are a number of reasons for the disappearance of the forest. Trees have been cut down for their wood. Areas have been cleared for farming. There are now cattle ranches and massive sugar and coffee plantations in places that once were forest.

Forest Conservation

It is vital for Brazil, and for the rest of the world, to find ways to reduce deforestation. This is beginning to happen. National parks and reserves have been set up. Over 103 million acres of forest are now legally protected, but many of the areas are so vast that it is almost impossible to police them properly. A more practical solution is necessary.

One answer to the problem has been the establishment of Extractive Reserves. Local people are allowed to collect renewable resources in Extractive Reserves. Many rain forest products, including rubber latex and brazil nuts, can be collected without causing damage. People also gather vines that are then made into hand brushes. Extractive Reserves help forest people earn money without destroying their environment.

Certifying wood is another method of protecting the forest. Only two trees are cut down for every two and a half acres of forest. Chains are used instead of heavy machinery. The impact on the forest is hardly noticeable, even from the air. This method of logging means that forest cover is not affected.

Source: Population Action International

▲ You can see how much of Brazil's forest has been destroyed in recent years.

◀ This man is holding the world's first guitar made from certified wood. The trees have been cut down far apart from each other so the forest is not damaged.

IN THEIR OWN WORDS

"My name is Paulo Kikuti. I am Chief Forest Officer for the Klabin Company, in the state of Paraná. Klabin is the largest paper and packaging company in Brazil. It owns large areas of forest at Telemacao Borba. Its plantation forests are a mixture of araucaria pine and eucalyptus trees, which it harvests every twenty years. Klabin also looks after areas of native forest left in between the plantations. These forests act as natural boundaries and protect the steep-sided waterways. Apart from the forests managed by Klabin, almost all the forests in Paraná have been converted to agricultural land. From the air, the large area of forest owned by Klabin can be seen as an island of trees surrounded by farmland."

Urban Environment

Almost all of Brazil's main cities are experiencing severe pollution. Many people are exposed to serious health risks from both the air and the water. Huge amounts of carbon monoxide and carbon dioxide are produced by the large number of cars on the road. Cubitão, which is a center for heavy metal industries, is the most polluted city in Brazil. It is closely followed by Rio de Janeiro.

▼ *This smelter in Cubitão is adding to the city's terrible air pollution. The level of pollution here is extremely harmful to human health.*

6

The Changing Population

In 1890, there were 14 million people in Brazil. By 2000, there were 170 million, making it the sixth most populous country in the world. However, Brazil has only 50 people for every square mile of its land. This means it has a low population density in comparison to many other countries.

The most populated areas are along the Atlantic coast and in the big cities. People who live in the interior of the country are few and far between, especially in the Center West states of Mato Grosso do Sul and do Norte, and the Amazon region.

Different People

The Brazilian population includes Amerindians, Portuguese, Africans, Japanese, Lebanese, Germans, Italians, and other Europeans. Brazil's first language is Portuguese, but many immigrants still speak their own languages. Spanish is the first language of almost every other South American country.

▲ *Look at how fast the Brazilian population has been growing.*

Africans

Between 1532 and 1850 it is estimated that more than five million slaves were brought from Africa. Slavery was finally abolished in 1888. Today, most of the people in the state of Bahía in the northeast are black Africans. Some of this region's most popular religions are based on the worship of African gods.

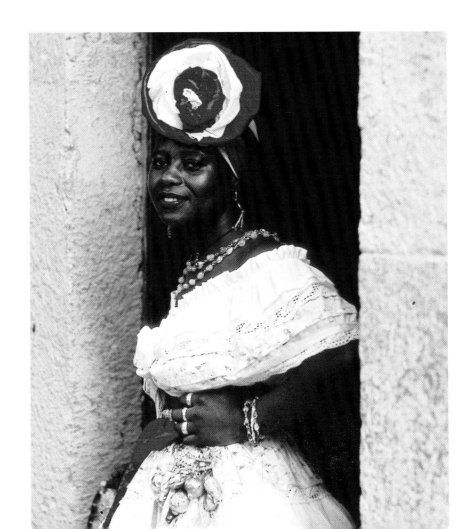

▶ *The African culture dominates the northeast. This woman from Bahía wears the traditional dress of the region.*

IN THEIR OWN WORDS

"My name is Sylvio Bittenberg. I live on a small farm with my wife and family in Pocone. I also run my own small sawmill. My parents emigrated from France to Brazil in the 1930s. They settled in the interior of the state of Santa Catarina. When I was young there was not much work where I lived, apart from farm labor. I decided to move to Mato Grosso twenty years ago. I wanted to try and get some land of my own. Now I have the farm and the sawmill. Seven people work for me. I am glad that I moved here."

Amerindians

The Amerindians were the original inhabitants of Brazil. Their population was devastated by the arrival of the Europeans, who brought new diseases with them. In the 16th century there were ten million Amerindians in Brazil. In 2001 there were approximately 200,000.

IN THEIR OWN WORDS

"My name is Bane Kaxinawa and I am 12 years old. I am a Kaxinawa Indian. The Kaxinawa people live in the Amazon rain forest close to the border of Peru. We grow manioc in our small gardens and we hunt and fish. We also collect rubber and vines. We make items such as hand brushes from the vines and sell them to tourists. Sometimes I help in our shop in the town of Rio Branco. I hope I will be able to work there when I am older."

Immigrants

After slavery was abolished, millions of people came from Europe, the Middle East, China, and Japan to work on the large plantations and in the gold mines. Many people in the south still speak German and Italian. São Paulo has the largest Japanese population outside Japan. Both Japanese and Portuguese are spoken in the city.

Urban Migration

Brazilian society was mainly rural at the beginning of the 20th century. Most people worked on farms or on coffee and sugar plantations. Others worked in the mines.

The situation has changed drastically over the last century. Large cities have developed and more and more people have moved to them in search of work. By 2001, two-thirds of Brazil's population lived in just nine major cities. The most urbanized regions are the southeast and the south.

Problems of overcrowding have arisen because so many people live in so few cities. In 1990, the government set up plans to encourage people to move out of the most crowded areas. Hundreds of thousands of people have since moved from the cities, particularly those in the northeast region. Most of them go to Amazonia or the sparsely populated Center West region.

Source: UNDP

▲ The percentage of Brazilians who live in cities is still going up.

◄ This building is in the city of Blumenau. Its design is typically Austrian. The people of Blumenau are white and speak German.

IN THEIR OWN WORDS

"My name is Seno Da Silva. I am one of the many thousands of people on the move in the northeast. My family and I have been traveling around the state of Bahía looking for a small piece of land on which we can grow food. All the good land is owned by the big farmers. The government has helped us survive by giving us food. We finally decided to settle on land that nobody seemed to be using. We cut down the trees and worked hard planting manioc, maize, and cocoa. If we can manage to stay on this land for seven years we can become its owners."

Children and the Elderly

The past forty years have seen family sizes fall sharply across all regions of Brazil. The average Brazilian couple had 6.3 children in 1960. In the year 2000, this average was down to 2.2 children. Meanwhile, the number of elderly in Brazil is increasing. In 1998 there were 2.2 million more people over the age of sixty than there were in 1993. This figure is still rising.

◀ *This retired fisherman is one of the growing number of elderly Brazilians. He spends his days making model boats out of balsa wood.*

7

Changes at Home

Family ties are very strong in Brazil. It is still common to find three generations of a family living in one house. Poorer families often have as many as five or six children. The grandparents help look after them while the parents work. Many children from poor families work instead of going to school.

Different Lifestyles

There is a lot of money in Brazil, but it is distributed very unevenly. The gap between rich and poor is vast. Some families in Brazil have luxurious homes in the cities and ranches in the countryside. Others lead lives similar to those in the poorest developing countries. Millions of people have no permanent homes. It is estimated that 4.4 million Brazilians live in *favelas* (city slums).

▲ *This favela is in the city of Manaus. Almost half of Brazil's favelas are in the cities of Rio de Janeiro and São Paolo.*

The different lifestyles in Brazil are not only caused by how much money people have. Each region of Brazil also has its own distinct way of life.

Life for the people of the Amazon has changed little in the last hundred years —although they might have satellite television now!

Many of the Europeans who emigrated to Brazil over the last 150 years settled in the south. Today, the region has whole communities that still live according to the traditions of the countries that their families came from.

The people in the southeast originate from many different parts of the world and there is an exciting mix of cultures in the region. Most people in the Center West live in cities. This region is gradually becoming richer. The majority of the population live in the northeast and are trying to make a living from the land. Many people here are extremely poor.

▲ Rio de Janeiro has beautiful apartments that overlook the beach. There is a huge contrast between this area and the city's slums.

IN THEIR OWN WORDS

"My name is Adrian Santo Mendes and I am 13 years old. I live with my family in Cachioera, which is a rubber tapper *colocacao* (settlement) in the Chico Mendes Extractive Reserve. The lives of the rubber tappers have improved a great deal in the last ten years. Most of the houses in Cachioera are bigger and more modern than they used to be.

"We have a satellite dish and a television in the village. We watch soccer matches on Saturday afternoons. I enjoy living here and I hope I can stay here when I finish school. I want to live and work in the forest like my father."

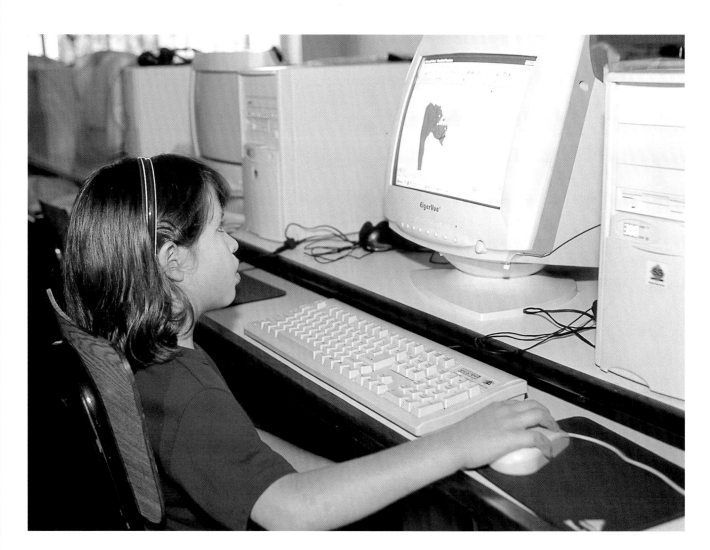

The Growing Middle Class

The people who make up the Brazilian middle-class live in the cities. They work in jobs such as office management or teaching. Most of them have to work long hours because it is so expensive to live in the cities. Their lives are similar to the lives of people in European and U.S. cities. City couples usually have small families of between one and three children.

Health

Brazilians have become much healthier since 1950. People have a better diet and access to improved healthcare. Brazilians are living longer because of these improvements. The average Brazilian is now expected to live more than 26 years longer than she or he did in 1950.

▲ *Children from wealthy and middle-class families often have access to a computer at home and at school.*

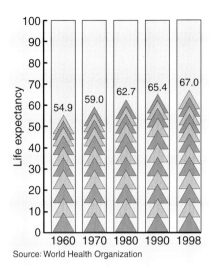

People's health in the different regions of Brazil varies dramatically. The people in the northeast die younger than people in other areas. Out of every 1,000 children born in this region, 57.9 will die before they reach the age of one. This is known as the infant mortality rate. The rate in the northeast is more than double that of the south, southeast, and Center West regions. Much of the population in the northeast is also malnourished. In the state of Alagoas, 16.3 percent of the population suffered from malnutrition in 1998. People in the south and southeast live longer and have the best hospitals in the country.

The government aims to provide the same healthcare for everyone. A vaccination program has been set up that is reducing disease in Brazil. Over 16 million children were vaccinated in 1999. This gave them protection against diseases including measles and poliomyelitis. Standards are improving throughout Brazil, but some states have more money to spend on healthcare than others.

Source: World Health Organization

▲ *This chart shows that Brazilians are living longer than in previous years.*

IN THEIR OWN WORDS

"My name is Alexandre Lorenzo. I live in Curitiba with my wife, Rachael, and my eight year old daughter, Daniella. We moved here from the small city of Cascavel five years ago. We came because there is more work here and Daniella can go to a better school.

"Today, I work in a hotel and also drive a taxi. We have a nice little house in the suburbs. We have decided to have only one child. I will work as hard as I can to give her a good start in life."

Women in the City

The traditional role for Brazilian women is to bring up the children and do the housework. This has changed in the last fifty years. More people are living in cities where life is expensive. Women often have to work to help support the family. Over forty percent of the workforce are now women. It is quite normal for men to take jobs where they are away from home for weeks at a time. Women are left to look after the children as well as having their own jobs. Sometimes other relatives can help, but often it is the oldest child who has to take care of his or her brothers and sisters. Divorce and separation are increasingly common.

Source: The Economist

▲ *See how many more women are going out to work in Brazil.*

◀ *This woman is cracking open the shells of brazil nuts. She will not be paid for any nuts that are broken.*

Girls have been receiving higher grades in school than boys for many years, but this is not rewarded when they enter the job market. A woman is still paid around 25 percent less than a man for doing the same job.

IN THEIR OWN WORDS

"My name is Aradne Sylvestre and I am 19 years old. I work in a clothing store in the center of Cuiabá. My family moved here from Rondonia when I was five–years–old. Cuiabá is still a man's city. There is only one female deputy in the whole state government. Fortunately, things are changing. More women are going into careers such as law. These types of job have all been done by men in the past. I can even imagine a female state governor here within the next twenty years. As for me, I am like many of the girls here. I like my job. I do want to have a family, but not until I have had a chance to earn some money and enjoy myself."

More women are going into higher education now. This means they can start careers in areas such as law, government, and medicine. In the past, these jobs would all have been done by men.

◄ Many villages have women's groups, which look after the rights of local women. This group is in the Atlantic Forest in the northeast.

◄ *There are primary schools in most of the villages in the Amazon's Flooded Forest.*

Education

Over 95 percent of children aged 7–14 go to elementary school, but many will not go on to high school. Children who live in the countryside often have to make a long journey to get to the secondary school. Some even have to live away from home. Most children in rural areas do not go to secondary school at all. In the northeast, 26.6 percent of the population are illiterate. People in the southeast are better educated and 92 percent of them can read and write.

IN THEIR OWN WORDS

"My name is Gladstone Marais Cavalho and I live in Manaus, which is the largest city in the Amazon. I am 13 years old and I have six brothers. I attend regular school in the afternoon and go to a musical instrument school from eight in the morning until lunchtime. I am learning how to make each part of a guitar. Eventually, I will know how to make a whole guitar by myself. When I finish school I want to have my own business. I hope to employ a few other people who can make musical instruments."

Leisure

Sports, and in particular soccer, are very popular in Brazil. Brazil has the largest soccer stadium in the world—the Maracana Stadium in Rio de Janeiro. Soccer is played throughout the country. The other main sports in Brazil are auto racing and tennis.

Many people spend their free time on the beach. They play volleyball and sunbathe. Brazilians like to look good and keeping fit is taken seriously.

▲ A huge crowd has come to watch a soccer game on a giant screen.

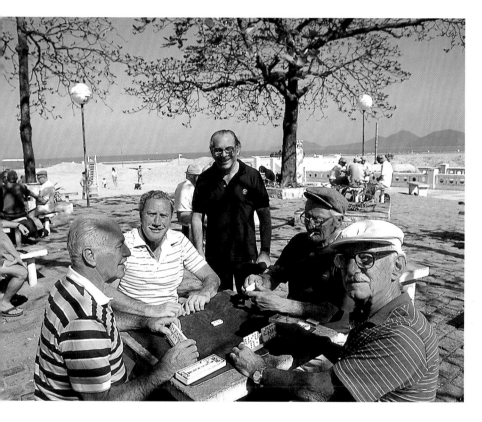

◄ These men are relaxing with a game of dominoes on the beach at São Paulo.

Carnival

The carnival is held every year in either February or March. A whole week of spectacular partying takes place all over the country.

The street parties in Rio de Janeiro are world famous. Rich and poor people join together in the parades and dancing. The fabulous costumes often take months to make. Many people travel to Brazil from other countries to join in the non-stop partying.

8

Changes at Work

Brazil was a rural society in 1900 and most people worked in farming or mining. Now most Brazilians work in a few large cities.

People have begun to move away from some of these cities in the last few years. The number of jobs in São Paulo decreased by around 600,000 between 1989 and 1997. Rio de Janeiro also lost 200,000 jobs in the same period.

There are two main reasons for this loss of work. One is that fewer people are needed in the factories because of modern production methods. Another important reason is that many businesses are moving out of these cities.

Where People Work

In 1989 most new businesses were started in cities in the southeast. Now more than half of all the money put into new businesses is spent outside of the traditional business centers. Companies are setting up in new towns and cities in different parts of the country.

▼ *Workers in São Paulo's city center traveling to work by subway.*

IN THEIR OWN WORDS

"My name is Fabio Martinez and I live in Curitiba. I work for a research company called LACTEC, at the Instituto de Tecnologia para Desenvovimento. High-tech businesses use our equipment to test their products.

"Here I am standing by a special machine that can produce the same electrical power as a bolt of lightning. Brazil often has very powerful thunderstorms. This machine is used to test new bits of electrical equipment to see if they are strong enough to withstand a lightning strike. We also offer other services, including chemical analysis and microprocessor design. Our customers include big companies such as Chrysler and Renault. Many companies set up in Curitiba because there are plenty of skilled workers, and companies like ours offer the services they need."

People are finding work in new parts of Brazil. In southern Brazil, the fastest-growing business areas are Minas Gerais and the smaller cities and towns in the states of São Paulo, Santa Catarina, Paraná, and Rio Grande do Sul. Many businesses are also setting up in the state of Ceará in the northeast. In the Center West, most of the new jobs are found in Mato Grosso.

▶ *Cuiabá is the main city in the Center West to which people are moving. Tourism is growing and there are many food processing factories here.*

Workers

There were an estimated 51.6 million people employed in Brazil in 1997. Over the past few years the number of jobs has fallen drastically. People have been forced to take whatever work they can find in order to survive. Many workers are not officially employed at all. This means they do not pay taxes. It also means they are often paid very low wages and have to work in bad conditions.

This informal work accounts for approximately one quarter of all jobs in Brazil today. Most maids, cleaners, and street vendors work unofficially. They received an average wage of just $75 a month in 1997. This is only just enough to survive in the cities.

There were 2.1 million children between 10 and 14 years old working in Brazil in 1998. This was a big improvement from 1993, when there were 3.4 million child workers. Slavery still continues in Brazil even though it has been illegal since 1888. There were more than 600 slaves in 1998.

▲ *These street vendors are selling goods in the city of Belém, Amazonia. They make very little money.*

◀ *A boy pans for gold near the mine at Pocone in Mato Grosso do Norte. Many children have to help support their families. They work instead of going to school.*

Agriculture

Many different crops can be grown in Brazil because it has a wide range of climates and soil types. The crops include coffee, cotton, corn, beans, rice, soy, sugarcane, and oranges. What is grown depends on demand from abroad. Brazil is the world's biggest orange producer and also the third-largest chicken producer. Its other main crops are coffee and soy. Livestock is also important. The cattle herd is the second largest in the world.

▼ *These cowboys work on a ranch in the state of São Paulo. There were a total of 163,470,000 animals in the Brazilian cattle herd in 1999.*

Agricultural Production

Production of soy, sugarcane, oranges, and cereal crops has increased dramatically since 1990. Overall production went up by nearly ten percent during 1998–99. However, international prices fell drastically in 1999. This means Brazil earned less money from agricultural exports even though it sold more produce.

Cropland has been expanding fast. Between 1980 and 1995, land was being converted to cropland at a rate of 4,250 square miles (11,000 square km) every year. By 1995, crops were being grown on 261,000 square miles (676,000 square km) of Brazil's land. Pasture crops, which produce feed for livestock, covered another 700,000 square miles (1.86 million square km).

New farming methods are increasing the productivity of the land. These include better soil conservation and improved irrigation of arid land. New technology is being brought in to the northeast. Until recently, most farming in this region had been done without machinery. Organic farming methods are also being used on some farms.

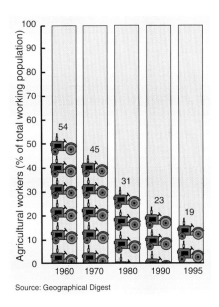

Source: Geographical Digest

▲ *The number of people needed to work on farmland has been decreasing for many years.*

◄ *This sugarcane field was once part of the Atlantic Forest. It is being burned after the harvest to kill off weeds and stop trees from regrowing.*

Mining

Brazil is one of the six major mining nations. Around 1,400 companies mine eighty different raw materials, including asbestos, bauxite, copper, iron ore, gold, tin, chromium, and graphite. The mining industry grew by 10.8 percent in 1998 and brought in $11.1 billion from exports.

▲ *This factory in Minas Gerais is processing aluminum. Aluminum is produced from bauxite, which is a clay-like substance found in the Earth's crust.*

IN THEIR OWN WORDS

"My name is Alaiso Brandi São Francisco and I live in Cuiabá. I am studying to become a mining engineer. Cuiabá was founded when gold was discovered here in the 16th century. Mining has been an important industry for the state of Mato Grosso do Norte ever since. I think the future of Mato Grosso will depend upon mining, agriculture, and tourism. I want to guarantee that I have a good job in twenty years' time."

Manufacturing Industries

Brazil is a highly industrialized country. There were 5.9 million people employed in manufacturing industries in 1997. The factories in Brazil produce cars, chemicals, communications equipment, electrical goods, processed food and drink, plastics, and pharmaceuticals.

The pharmaceuticals industry is an area that could bring vast sums of money into Brazil in the future. The plants in Brazil's forests are being studied and new products developed from them. A whole new range of health products is already available locally in Brazil.

Car production is another of Brazil's most important industries. The number of cars produced increased from 1.4 million in 1994 to 2 million in 1997. It is predicted that Brazil will be the world's fifth-largest car producer by 2005, producing 2.6 million cars every year.

▲ *These dried medicinal plants have been collected from the araucaria pine forest in the southern state of Paraná.*

Service Industries

Service industries include banking, computer programming, restaurants, retail, and tourism. They also include transportation and garbage collection. Businesses in this sector do not produce any goods.

IN THEIR OWN WORDS

"My name is José da Silva and I live in Goiania with my wife and two children. I have a job in Brasilia laying the grass and the pavements around a new shopping center. A huge restaurant is being built behind me (*right*) and my coworker. I work away from my family for two weeks without a break. Then I have two days at home before doing another two weeks' work. I miss my family, but I have to earn money where I can."

A large service sector is a sign that a country is doing well. It means people have money to spend. More people work in services than in any other industry in Brazil. Services in Brazil make more money than the total amount made by agriculture and manufacturing.

Telecommunication companies are among the fastest-growing businesses in Brazil. There were fewer than one million mobile telephones used in 1994. By 1999 the figure was approaching 11 million.

Transportation companies are very important to Brazil because it is such a huge country. There are 94,000 buses in Brazil and they carry approximately fifty million passengers. The airlines are another successful service industry. They generated more than $2 billion in 1998.

▲ *This modern shopping center in the Amazonian city of Belém is a sign of the city's increasing wealth.*

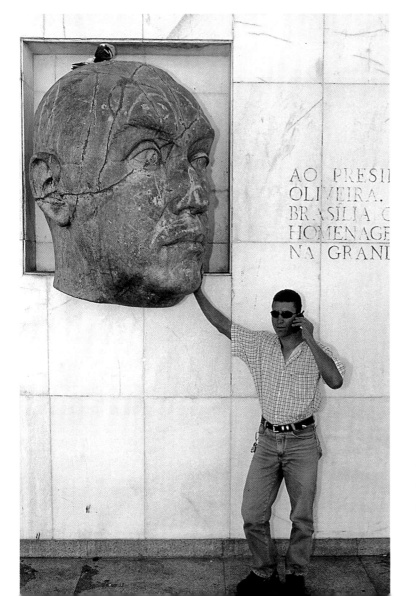

◄ *This young taxi driver works in Brasilia. He is one of the many mobile telephone users who are making the Brazilian telecommunications industry so successful.*

9 The Way Ahead

Brazil is often called the "sleeping giant." It is a huge country with vast natural resources, but it has not quite "woken up" to its own potential. Brazil is rich in oil, gold, and iron ore and has large areas of productive farmland. It also has a large, energetic, and young population. The country seems to have all the ingredients for a bright future. However, Brazil has some serious problems it has to address if it is going to be successful in the 21st century.

Problems to Be Overcome

Brazil developed rapidly in the 20th century and it now has the eighth largest economy in the world. Business people are making increasingly large sums of money, but the benefits of these new riches have not reached many parts of the population. The divide between rich and poor in Brazil is one of the largest in the world.

▲ The future looks bright for this girl, but many other young Brazilians will suffer if the country does not address its problems.

◄ The Iguaçu Falls are in southern Brazil, on the border with Argentina and Uruguay. The Falls are a symbol of Brazil's powerful potential.

Brazil also has the largest foreign debt of any country. The government borrowed money from other countries to pay for new development projects. The projects were successful at first, but the huge loan repayments are crippling the country.

Serious environmental problems also need to be resolved. Rain forest destruction needs to be stopped and pollution of air and water supplies must be reduced.

Brazil has come a long way in the last century, but it must now address some of its most pressing problems. If successful, Brazil could become the most powerful country in the southern hemisphere.

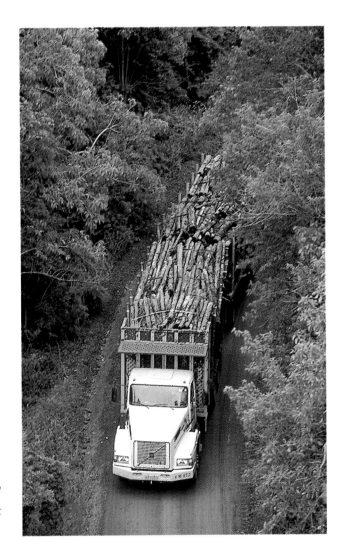

▶ *These logs are from a plantation forest in the southern state of Paraná. Plantations help reduce demand on natural forests.*

IN THEIR OWN WORDS

"My name is João Augusto Fortes and I work in Rio de Janeiro. My job is to promote rain forest products made from natural rubber. The rubber tapper co-operatives in the Amazon communicate with my company over the Internet. They collect rubber latex and process it into 'vegetable leather.' This is made into items such as bags in Rio de Janeiro.

Our products are sold all over the world using the Internet. Our business is to make money out of natural products without destroying the forest. We think this is the way forward for Brazil."

Glossary

Cassava A large potato-like root vegetable. It is the staple diet of Amazonian Indians and is eaten by almost all Brazilians.

Cerrado The Brazilian word for lightly-forested savannah.

Cooperative A business that is owned and run by the people who work in it.

Deforestation The clearance of trees, either for wood or so the land can be used for another purpose.

Economy All the business that goes on in a country.

Ecotourism Visiting places to experience their natural beauty.

Emigrate Go to live in another country.

Escarpment An inland cliff or steep slope.

Export Sell goods to another country.

Extractive Reserve An area of forest that is protected but where local people can collect renewable products such as fruit, nuts, and rubber latex.

Hydroelectric power Electricity generated by using the power of water.

Illiterate Unable to read and write.

Immigrants People who come to live in a country from abroad.

Import Buy goods from another country.

Independence Freedom to rule oneself.

Irrigation Artificial system of water supply to farmland.

Malnourished Suffering from a lack of nutrition due to lack of food or a poor diet.

Manioc The Brazilian word for cassava.

Metal alloy A mix of two or more metals.

Migration Moving from one area or country to another.

Pharmaceuticals Drugs (medicinal).

Plantation A large estate where trees or plants are grown so that wood or other produce, such as coffee, can be sold.

Plateau An area of high, flat land.

Poliomyelitis A crippling childhood disease.

Populous Containing many people.

Prairie Treeless grassland.

Rain forest Dense tropical forest where there is high rainfall.

Rights Those things due to a person under law.

Rubber latex Milky white sap (liquid) collected by scratching the bark of the rubber tree. It is heated until it forms a solid block.

Rubber tapper A person who collects rubber latex.

Rural Countryside.

Savannah Open grassland in the tropics or subtropics with few trees or bushes.

Smelter A factory that extracts metals from metal ores by heating.

Southern hemisphere The half of the world that lies south of the Equator.

Urban Built up, as in a town or city.

Wetland Land that is permanently soaked with water—often by floods.

Further Information

Books

Bender, Evelyn. *Brazil (Major World Nations Series)*. Broomall, PA: Chelsea House, 1998.

Cruxton, J. Bradley, editor. *Discovering the Amazon Rainforest*. New York: Oxford University Press, 1999.

Draffen, Andrew and Nick Selby. *Brazil*. Oakland, CA: Lonely Planet, 1998.

Heinrichs, Ann. *Brazil*. Danbury, CT: Children's Press, 1997.

Levine, Robert M. and John J. Crocitti, editors. *The Brazil Reader: History, Culture, Politics*. Durham, NC: Duke University Press, 1999.

McKay, Susan. *Brazil (Festivals of the World)*. Milwaukee, WI: Gareth Stevens, 1997.

Useful Addresses

Friends of the Earth
1025 Vermont Avenue, NW, Suite 300
Washington, D.C. 20005-6303
Website: www.foe.org

Oxfam America
1112 16th St. NW, Suite 600
Washington, D.C. 20036
Website: www.oxfamamerica.org

World Wildlife Fund
1250 24th Street, N.W.
Washington, D.C. 20037
Website: www.worldwildlife.org

WWF in Brazil
Website: www.wwf.org.br/wwfeng/

Brazilian Embassy
3006 Massachusetts Avenue, N.W.
Washington, D.C. 20008
Website: www.brasilemb.org

Websites

www.brazilfutebol.com
Official Site for the Brazilian Football (Soccer) Federation. Get news, scores, player statistics, team information, World Cup history facts about Brazil, and more.

www.oxfam.org.uk/coolplanet/kidsweb/ world/Brazil/brazhome.htm
Oxfam Cool Planet's Brazil. Learn about life in Brazil today including the people, history, geography, and more.

www.lonelyplanet.com/destinations/south _america/brazil/
Lonely Planet Destinations—Brazil. Learn all about Brazil and see some great photos.

www.uol.com.br/allbrazilianmusic
All Brazilian Music. A guide to Brazilian music styles, artists' biographies and discographies, and news.

Websites for Statistics on Brazil

www.undp.org
United Nations Development Program (UNDP)

www.unicef.org
United Nations Children's Fund (UNICEF)

www.odci.gov/cia/publications/factbook
CIA World Factbook

www.fao.org
Food and Agricultural Association of the United Nations (FAO)

Index

Numbers in **bold** are pages where there is a photograph or an illustration